Hey! Christians Have a Sense of Humor, Too!

He that is of a merry heart hath a continual feast.
Proverbs 15:15

Hey! Christians Have a Sense of Humor, Too!

Lighthearted Jokes & Sayings

Hey! Christians Have a Sense of Humor, Too!
ISBN 978-0-9895802-5-0
Published by Product Concept Mfg., Inc.
2175 N. Academy Circle #200, Colorado Springs, CO 80909

Written and Compiled by Patricia Mitchell
in association with Product Concept Mfg., Inc.

All scripture quotations are from the King James version
of the Bible unless otherwise noted.

Scriptures taken from the Holy Bible,
New International Version®, NIV®.
Copyright © 1973, 1978, 1984 by Biblica, Inc.™
Used by permission of Zondervan.
All rights reserved worldwide.
www.zondervan.com

Sayings not having a credit listed are contributed by writers
for Product Concept Mfg., Inc. or in a rare case,
the author is unknown.

Who says that Christians can't smile?

Not God, that's for sure. And if you doubt that the Creator doesn't have a sense of whimsy, just picture an aardvark and platypus resting beneath a baobab tree!

God richly blesses His people with a taste for humor and gives us the gift of laughter to enjoy and to share. With clean, uplifting, and God-honoring chuckles, we not only refresh ourselves, but encourage others to relax and see life's lighter side. What's not to smile about that?

Here's a little collection of jokes, anecdotes, quips, and cartoons to get your smile going. You'll find funnies about church and family life, and about everyday living. If you're feeling a bit down today, let a few of these pages lift you up. If you've already got the giggles, take a selection of chuckles with you to share with someone today!

Laughter is a blessing—spread it around!

HOLY HUMOR

"I've just created a 24-hour period of alternating light and darkness," God told one of His angels. "Wonderful!" exclaimed the angel. "So what are You going to do now?"

"I think I'll call it a day," God replied.

•

A parishioner noticed that the pastor kept three pairs of glasses on his desk. When she asked why, he replied: "I need one pair for distance, one pair for reading, and one pair to look for the other two."

•

Pastor had sanitary hot-air hand dryers installed in the church restrooms. The next month, however, he called to have them removed.

The first parishioner who saw that the dryers had disappeared asked the pastor why, as it seemed they were working just fine. Pastor turned to him and said, "I liked them, too, but last week when I went into the men's restroom, someone had put a sign above the dryer that read, 'For a sample of this week's sermon, push the button.'"

LET'S NOT GO THERE

One evening Dad asked his young son to go downstairs to his workbench in the basement and get him a hammer. His son blanched and stood wide-eyed with fear. "What's the matter, son?" his dad asked.

"Ummm, I don't want to go down into the basement," his son replied in a trembling voice. "It's dark where the hammers are and I can't reach the light."

His dad smiled and said reassuringly, "All you have to do is grab the first hammer you find. And besides, Jesus is everywhere, and He's down there, too."

Hesitantly the boy ventured downstairs and stood at the door of the basement. He opened it a crack and called, "Hey, Jesus! If You're down there, could you hand me a hammer, please?"

School Daze

A middle-school teacher injured his back over the summer. When school started, he still was wearing a plaster cast around his upper body, but it wasn't visible under his shirt and jacket.

On the first day of school, as he was explaining classroom rules to a group of unruly fifth graders, his tie blew in his face, which caused an uproar of laughter. The teacher calmly walked over to the window and closed it. Then he picked up a stapler from his desk and appeared to staple his tie to his chest!

The room became so quiet you could hear a pin drop. The entire year passed without any discipline problems.

•

A kindergarten teacher spread out a map of the world in front of her class. "Tommy," she said, "please come to the map and find North America." Dutifully Tommy approached the map and put his hand on the correct continent.

"Very good!" the teacher beamed as Tommy returned to his seat. "Now class," she said, "who discovered North America?"

Lisa's hand shot up. "Tommy!" she shouted.

Favorite hymns for...

Gossips: "I Love to Tell the Story"

Formally attired men: "Blest Be the Tie That Binds"

Lost drivers: "Guide Me, O Thou Great Jehovah"

Clock watchers: "Moment by Moment"

Moms on first day of school: "Peace, Blessed Peace"

Hikers: "Go Tell It on the Mountain"

HD TV watchers: "All Things Bright and Beautiful"

Golfers: "There Is a Green Hill Far Away"

Beachgoers: "I Saw Three Ships"

Bow WOW!

At church one Sunday, Marv started bragging about his Christian dog. "How in the world can a dog be a Christian?" Bill asked skeptically.

"Come and see," said Marv. That afternoon, Bill went over to Marvin's house to meet his amazing canine.

"Watch this," the proud dog owner said as a perky brown mutt trotted over. Addressing the dog, Marv said, "Let us pray." At this command, the dog sat down, put his front paws together, and lifted his eyes to heaven.

"Impressive," admitted Bill. "What else can he do?"

"Go get the Bible," said Marv to the dog. With that, the dog immediately went to a desk, opened a drawer, and pulled out a Bible. He brought the book to his master and opened it to John 3:16.

"Truly amazing!" exclaimed Bill. "But can he follow regular dog commands?"

"Huh," said Marv. "Never asked him to." Looking at the dog, he said, "Heel!" With that, the dog stood on his hind legs, put his paw on Marv's forehead, and bowed his head in prayer.

HOLY HUMOR

During the announcements one Sunday, the pastor said that there would be a board meeting in the back of the church immediately after the service. At the appointed time, the board members gathered, but when the pastor approached, he saw that a visitor was standing among them. "Brother," he said, "this meeting is for the board only."

"Yes, reverend, I know that," the man replied, "and I came because I reckon I'm about as bored as anyone."

•

A boy was watching a distant thunderstorm with his father. As streaks of light shot across the sky, his father remarked on the awesome power of God's creation and how fast a lightning bolt can travel. Sonny thought a minute and then said, "Dad, I think that lightning would travel a lot faster if it didn't zigzag."

•

Did you hear about the town's ministers who got together and formed a bowling team?
They called themselves the Holy Rollers.

Seen in the church parking lot...

Corduroy pillows make headlines!

Change is inevitable, except from vending machines.

Do vegetarians eat animal crackers?

A balanced diet is a brownie in each hand.

Be alert! The world needs more lerts.

I once had a handle on life, but it broke.

Sorry I'm driving so closely in front of you.

Never forget: You are one of those who can be fooled some of the time.

"For some reason I'm feeling a little down
in the mouth today."

Just Horsing Around

A lone tourist wandered far off the beaten track. After a week of meandering through a seemingly endless desert, he finally came across a small house sitting by itself next to an oasis. Elated, the man knocked on the door of the house. A wizened man, a hermit, answered.

The tourist explained his predicament, and the hermit offered him food, water, and a place to sleep. As the nearest town was fifty miles away, the man stayed with the hermit several days while he recouped from his ordeal. When he was ready to leave, the man asked the hermit for directions back to civilization.

The hermit pointed him in the right direction and described landmarks along the way. Then he said, "Since it's so far, perhaps you'd like to borrow my horse." The man gladly accepted the hermit's generous offer.

As he brought the horse from behind his house, the hermit said, "Now there's something you need to know about this horse. You must say 'Thank God' when you want him to go and 'Amen' when you want him to stop."

The man, however, was so eager to get going that he paid scant attention to the hermit's instructions.

Thanking his host, he mounted the horse, and with a sigh of relief he said, "Thank God!" The horse started trotting in the direction of the town.

When the man spied the first landmark, a gnarled tree that had been hit by lightning, he exclaimed, "Thank God!" The horse picked up the pace considerably.

Soon the man saw the second landmark, a rock shaped like a man's profile. "Thank God!" he yelled. The horse broke into a full gallop.

Then the third landmark, a bluff, came into view. That is where the hermit had told the man to turn north and travel parallel to the cliff. "Oh, thank God, thank God!" the man exclaimed. At that, the horse galloped even faster, straight toward the precipice. Terrified, the man shouted, "Whoa! Whoa! Stop!" as he pulled frantically on the reins. But the horse kept going.

Just in the nick of time, the man remembered the hermit's instructions and screamed, "Amen! Amen!" The horse came to a halt three feet from the edge of the cliff. Wiping the sweat from his brow, the man looked up to heaven and cried in a loud voice, "Thank God!!"

In the Sunday bulletin...

Deacon Jones spoke briefly, much to the delight of the congregation.

The church picnic will take place at 2 p.m., with prayer and medication to follow.

Everyone invited to hear Pastor Wells speak on the topic, "How to Get to Heaven." Transportation available from Grand Shopping Center parking lot.

The class on prophecy has been canceled due to unforeseen circumstances.

When Pastor's sermon comes to an end, the congregation will join in singing, "Break Forth into Joy."

Low self-esteem support group meeting this evening at 7. Please use back door.

The choir invites you to join them this Tuesday at 7:30 p.m. for Christmas practice. They need all the help they can get!

Remember, there's extra seating upstairs in the baloney.

UNWELCOME VISITORS

Three pastors were having lunch. One said, "I'm having a problem keeping bats out of the church building. They're in the bell tower, in my office, in the hallways, and even in the sanctuary. I can't get rid of them!"

"Let me tell you about the bats that have invaded my church," the second pastor said. "They're hanging from the ceiling, the rafters, and the walls. In the evening, they're flying around all over the place! I've tried all kinds of traps, but nothing seems to work."

"Here's what I did with my bat problem," the third pastor said. "I simply made them members of my congregation and gave each critter an offering envelope. Haven't seen one of 'em since."

WIT AND WISDOM

Cheerfulness keeps up a kind
of daylight in the mind, and fills it with
a steady and perpetual serenity.

Joseph Addison

●

Live your life in such a way
that you wouldn't be ashamed to sell the family
parrot to the town gossip.

Will Rogers

●

A person without a sense of humor
is like a wagon without springs—
jolted by every pebble in the road.

Henry Ward Beecher

●

Wit is the salt of conversation,
not the food.

William Hazlitt

If...

You melt dry ice, can you swim in it
without getting wet?

Baby pigs are called piglets, why aren't
baby bulls called bullets, and baby chicks
called chicklets?

Boomerangs always come back to you,
why throw them in the first place?

Someone eats all the pudding, how are
we going to prove anything?

Quitters never win and winners never quit,
then why do people say, "Quit while you're ahead"?

There's mileage, yardage, and footage,
why don't we have inchage?

Olive oil comes from olives, where does
baby oil come from?

Doubting Thomas

One afternoon while hiking, Thomas stumbled and fell over the side of a steep cliff. Before he hit bottom, however, he managed to grab hold of a tree branch. Dangling precariously over the canyon, he shouted, "Lord, can You hear me?"

"Yes, my son," replied the Lord, "I can hear you."

"Can you help me?" the man cried.

"Of course!" said the Lord. "Just let go of the branch and I'll catch you."

Thomas thought for a moment, lifted his eyes to heaven, and pleaded: "Lord, can anyone else hear me?"

Business as Usual

"Doctor!" the irate patient screamed,
"you have a nerve charging me three hundred
dollars just to paint my throat!"
"So what do you want for three hundred dollars?"
the doctor said. "Wallpaper?"

•

A sales associate decided on a career change,
so he became a police officer. After several months
had passed, a friend asked the man how he liked
his new job. "Well," he said, "the pay could be
better, the hours are long, and it can be dangerous, but what I like about it is that the customer
is always wrong!"

•

The pastor of a large church always scheduled
meetings for his administrative staff at 4:30
on Friday afternoons. When an assistant pastor
joined the staff, he asked his new boss why he
chose such an odd time for meetings.
"Two reasons," the pastor replied.
"One: No one asks me any questions; and two:
No one argues with my proposals."

The Pearly Gates

A man was stranded in a mountain cabin during a terrible rainstorm. When the water flooded his cabin, he crawled up on the roof and watched the water as it rose higher and higher. He began to pray fervently. As he was praying, two guys in a boat came along. "Hop in, pal," they yelled. "We're here to save you!"

"No need," the man shouted back, "because I'm a believer and I know that God will rescue me!" The men looked at each other, shrugged, and rowed to the next cabin.

Soon, with the waters still rising, a canoe appeared and a man threw out a life preserver. "Grab it!" the man in the canoe yelled, "and I'll pull you in!"

Again the man on the roof refused the offer, declaring that God would save him. When the water reached the tips of the man's toes, a helicopter hovered overhead. "Climb the ladder!" the pilot screamed. "This is your last chance to get out before you drown!"

"Don't worry, I won't drown," the man called back, "because God will save me!"

The helicopter left. The waters rose, and the man drowned.

Sopping wet and red with anger, the man walked up to the Pearly Gates. "What's the meaning of this?" he asked St. Peter. "I've been a believer all my life! I put my faith in God and I trusted Him to save me from the flood!"

"What are you complaining about?" St. Peter replied. "God sent you two boats and a helicopter!"

Play It Again!

One Saturday, the church treasurer confronted the pastor with a $5,000 budget shortfall. Distressed, the minister spent a sleepless night thinking about the best way to motivate his tight-fisted congregation to increase their offerings. He was preoccupied with the subject on Sunday morning when the organist called to tell him she had the flu, but had arranged for a substitute.

The substitute arrived shortly before the service was to start. The pastor handed her the order of service, and then said, "I have a special announcement to make after the service, so please think of something to play when I'm done."

When announcement time came, the pastor stood before the congregation and said, "Brothers and sisters, due to unexpected repairs and cost increases, our church is in debt. Therefore I'm asking each family to prayerfully consider a gift of $100 or more. If you can do this, please stand up."

At that moment, the organist launched into "The Star-Spangled Banner."

That Sunday, the budget was balanced.

Driving Privileges

Sam had just received his driver's license. Eager to get on the road, he asked his pastor-dad about using the family car. His dad saw an opportunity to motivate his son to make some needed changes in his personal life. "I'll tell you what," Dad said. "You bring your grades up, attend Bible class regularly, and get your hair cut, we'll talk."

Six weeks later, Sam returned to his father and again asked about the use of the car. "Sam, you've made great progress! You've aced your exams and you've been present every week for Bible class. I'm proud of you! But I asked you to get your hair cut, too, and you haven't done that."

Sam looked down at the floor and replied, "Well, Dad, I've given that a lot of thought during Bible class. Samson had long hair, didn't he? So did Moses and Abraham and Noah. Even Jesus wore his hair long."

"You're right, son, they did," his dad said, "and you'll remember that they walked everywhere they went."

Better with Age

"She's in great shape for someone her age,"
said a woman to her friend, not a little enviously.
"Well," replied her catty friend, "way back when
she was born, things were built to last."

•

The most frustrating thing about reaching your
senior years is finding high-priced antiques and
remembering items just like them that you sold for
50¢ at a garage sale twenty years ago.

•

"Growing older isn't so bad," Liz confided to her
daughter, "but maintenance sure takes a lot more
effort than it used to."

•

Two neighbors had a spat, and they decided to
take their argument for arbitration. Both women
appeared in front of the mediator who looked
at them and said, "Okay, I understand there's
a problem. Let's hear from the oldest person
first." Neither had anything to say, and the
session ended.

IN THE BEGINNING

One day a famous scientist decided that there was no longer any need on Earth for God. And the man proceeded to tell Him so.

"God, You're completely irrelevant," he declared. "It's the 21st century, and people have made great strides in the fields of medicine, astronomy, and geoscience. So it's time You stop insisting that people pray to You and believe in Your power."

God listened, and then He replied: "Well, before I distance myself from the world, let's have a contest. How about we both create a human being?"

"Sure!" the scientist said smugly, reaching for a test tube in his lab.

"Wait, wait!" God said. "We're going to do this the way I did back in the Garden of Eden."

"OK, no problem," the scientist said as he put the test tube back on his shelf. He walked outside, bent down and picked up a handful of dirt.

God looked at him. "No, no, no," He said. "You have to come up with your own dirt!"

In Sunday School

The Sunday school class listened as their teacher described how Lot's wife looked back on the destruction of Sodom and turned into a pillar of salt. Meg's hand went up. "My mom looked back once while driving," the girl announced, "and she turned into a telephone pole."

•

In Sunday school, after a lesson on Jesus' many miracles, the teacher asked, "Is there anything God can't do?"

"There sure is, Miss Miller," one tyke said. "No matter what He does, He can't please everybody."

•

Standing in front of the inn, the young Sunday schooler playing Joseph in the Christmas program forgot his lines. From the side of the stage, his teacher prompted him, saying, "Remember, you and Mary have traveled a long time, and you're tired and thirsty. What do you say to the innkeeper?" The boy brightened and shouted, "Excuse me, sir, but can you give us some lemonade?

ADAM AND EVE

After Adam and Eve ate the forbidden fruit, their eyes were opened, and they saw that they were naked. Adam quickly pulled a fig leaf from a tree and covered himself. Eve grabbed one, too, and covered herself. Then she tried on a maple leaf, then a sycamore leaf, then an oak leaf...

•

The previous Sunday, little Billy heard about how God created man out of the dust of the ground, and how He created Eve from one of Adam's ribs. Later in the week, while playing outside, he developed a pain in his side. He turned to his friend with a serious look on his face and said, "My ribs hurt. I think I'm going to have a wife."

•

With great reverence, a little boy opened the family Bible that always sat on the living room table. As he was carefully turning the pages, a big leaf slipped out and fell to the floor. He picked it up and studied it. "Mom!" he shouted, "I think I just found Adam's clothes!"

VOCAL PETS

A boy went into the pet shop and asked the manager: "Do you have any puppies going cheap?" "No, son, I don't," the manager said. "All the puppies here go woof, woof."

•

His parents agree he can have a pet, provided the pet is a fish. Elated, the boy walks into a pet store and happens on a brightly colored fish called a parrot fish. The shop owner, a man known for his tall tales, informs the boy that he can teach this fish to sing.

The boy takes home the fish, names it Pavarotti, and begins to teach the fish to sing. After several weeks, however, the boy meets a friend and expresses disappointment with his pet. His friend chides him: "I can't believe you thought a parrot fish could actually sing!"

"He does sing!" the boy protests. "In fact, he sings all night long! But he sings off-key, and you have no idea how hard it is to tune a fish!"

Something Fishy Here

The baby octopus complained to the Creator
about being an octopus. God asked,
"What's so bad about being an octopus?"
The octopus replied, "Do You have any idea how
long it takes me to wash my hands before dinner?"

●

Teach a man to fish, and he'll eat for the rest of
his life. Teach a fish to learn, and soon they'll be
swimming around in schools.

●

A man went to the seafood counter at his local
supermarket carrying a trout under his arm.
"Do you make fish cakes?"
the man asked the clerk at the counter.
"Yes, we do," said the clerk.
"Great!" replied the man,
"because I need one for his birthday!"

●

"Dolphins are much smarter than people,"
a boy proclaimed to his friend as they were
watching a performance. "After all, in a couple
hours they can train someone to stand at the side
of a pool and feed them!"

Out Shopping

A man went into the hardware store and asked the assistant for a box of nails. "How long do you want them?" the assistant asked.

"They're for my roof," the man replied, "and I plan to keep them."

●

A woman angrily entered the flooring outlet where she had recently ordered a large living room carpet. "When I bought it, you assured me that the carpet would be in mint condition!" she shouted to the sales assistant.

"It is in mint condition," the associate replied. "There's a perfect hole in the middle."

●

A man entered a discount shop and asked the clerk: "Honestly, is everything here only a dollar?"

"Yes, sir," the clerk replied, "every item you see is priced at one dollar."

"That being the case," the man said as he handed her a dollar, "I'll take the cash register."

Holy Humor

A devout rancher's Bible fell out of his pocket while he was mending the fence at the far end of the pasture. Three weeks later, the rancher was working outside when a cow came up to him with the Bible in her mouth. Delighted, the rancher took the Bible from the cow's mouth, raised his eyes to heaven and exclaimed, "It's a miracle!"

"Not really," replied the cow as she sauntered off. "Your name's on the cover."

•

One day an ape escaped from the city zoo. A huge search team scoured the neighborhood for him, and alerts were broadcast over radio and TV. Finally a librarian spotted him sitting in the back of the library with two books open in front of him: the Bible and a tome on evolution. "What are you doing?" she asked the animal.

He looked up and said, "I'm trying to find out whether I'm my brother's keeper or my keeper's brother."

•

Two fellows were walking out of Bible class one Sunday. "I'm really glad I'm getting to understand the Bible better," one said. "You know, I always thought Sodom and Gomorrah were husband and wife."

"To be honest," his friend replied, "I always thought the Epistles were wives of the apostles."

Ups and Downs of Life

A parachutist jumped out of a plane, but when he pulled on his cord to open the chute, nothing happened. As he frantically attempted to fix the chute on his way down, he saw another man on his way up. "Say," the parachutist shouted, "you wouldn't know anything about parachutes, would you?" "No," yelled the man. "Do you know anything about gas grills?"

•

As the plane was taxiing down the runway, the flight attendant advised passengers to take some gum. "It will prevent your ears from popping as we gain altitude," she said. At the destination, everyone got off except one man. "Do you need assistance?" the attendant asked him. "Please speak up!" he shouted. "I can't hear a thing with this gum in my ears!"

•

As one elevator said to the other, "I think I'm coming down with something."

•

"This is my first time flying," a woman said to the pilot as she boarded the plane. "You'll get us down safely, won't you?" "I can assure you of one thing, ma'am," the pilot replied. "We've never left anyone up there!"

So True...

Flexible people never get bent out of shape.

It's hard to tell the age of someone whose spirit remains young.

Life would be easier if it came with an "undo" key.

Great ideas need landing gear as well as wings.

Worry is interest paid by those who borrow trouble.

It's only by doing that we discover what we're able to do.

Don't wish upon a star...reach for one!

Attitude is everything, so might as well pick a good one.

Q&A Time: Critters

Why are frogs always happy?
Because they eat whatever bugs them.

What did the pony say when he woke up with a sore throat?
Very little because he was so horse.

What should you do if you see two snails having a fight?
Leave them alone and let them slug it out.

What did the beaver say to the tree?
It's been nice gnawing you.

What are the smartest bees?
Spelling bees.

How do you get down from an elephant?
You don't; you get down from a duck.

What happened to the snail that lost its shell?
It got sluggish.

'Tis the Season

The parents of twins couldn't get over how different they were from each other. One, Jill, was a pessimist through and through. No matter what her parents gave her, she found something wrong with it. The more they tried to please her, the more dissatisfied she became. The other, Jane, was just the opposite—an optimist; a pleasure to do for, buy for, and dote on, because she was so accepting and grateful.

Before buying Christmas presents one year, the parents asked a counselor how to handle gift-giving in the best possible way. "If you can afford it, buy Jill what she asks for," he suggested. "But you can get Jane anything, even a bag of manure, and she'd be happy."

The parents followed the counselor's advice to the letter—buying Jill a bike and Jane a bag of manure. On Christmas morning, the twins opened their gifts.

"Oh, a bike," moaned Jill. "I'll probably fall off of it and break my legs. Or it'll get stolen when I park it. Or I'll get hit by a car and have to be taken to the hospital."

Jane, however, was busy peering at the manure. "Wow!" she exclaimed. "I think I got a pony, but I haven't quite found him yet."

Favorite songs in Bible times...

Adam and Eve: "Strangers in Paradise"

Lazarus: "The Second Time Around"

Elijah: "Up, Up and Away"

Samson: "Hair"

Moses: "The Wanderer"

Joshua: "Good Vibrations"

Daniel: "The Lion Sleeps Tonight"

Job: "I've Got a Right to Sing the Blues"

Noah: "Raindrops Keep Falling on My Head"

Quick Quips

Good things that come into your life by serendipity are simply times that God chooses to remain anonymous.

God promises a safe landing, not a calm voyage.

Don't let stress get you down! Remember, Moses started out as a basket case.

Swallowing your pride rarely leads to indigestion.

If God is your co-pilot, swap seats immediately!

Opportunity knocks once, but temptation bangs on your door forever.

Many Christians are ready and willing to serve God, but only as advisors.

All for Love

One evening while they were sitting in the park
holding hands, a girl said to her boyfriend:
"Do you love me?"
"Of course I do," he replied.
"Then whisper something soft and sweet
in my ear," she said.
He leaned over and gently whispered,
"Lemon meringue pie."

●

A woman signed up with a computer dating
service. Under "likes," she put water sports and
formal attire. A day later the computer matched
her up with a penguin.

●

A little girl announced to her mother, "Mom, when
I grow up, I'm going to marry the boy next door."
"Really?" her mom replied. "And why is that?"
"Because you won't allow me to cross the street."

●

Sally suspected that her boyfriend had commitment
issues. Her doubts were confirmed one Saturday
when they were playing tennis. Instead of saying
"fifteen-love," he announced "fifteen-like-you-a-lot."

Have you heard the one about...

The skunk who went to church every Sunday?
He even had his own pew!

The novice cook who bought a cured ham?
She spent all afternoon trying to find out what it had.

The tomcat who lost his tail?
That's what brought him to the retail store.

The vacationer who would leave nothing to chance?
She even brought along some sand.

The man who fell into an upholstery machine?
But don't worry—he's fully recovered.

The guy who asked his gal if he could change her name to his?
When she said "yes," he started calling her Bruce.

Be Happy

Life is a shipwreck,
but we must not forget to sing in the lifeboats.

Voltaire

•

Drag your thoughts away from your troubles...
by the ears, by the heels,
or any other way you can manage it.

Mark Twain

•

If you see ten troubles coming down the road,
you can be sure that nine will run into
the ditch before they reach you.

Calvin Coolidge

•

If the skies fall, one may hope to catch larks.

François Rabelais

•

Whatever tears one may shed,
in the end one always blows one's nose.

Heinrich Heine

Fun Puns

What do you get when you divide the circumference of a pumpkin by its diameter?
Pumpkin pi.

What happened to the guy who ate all the Christmas decorations?
He came down with tinselitis.

What did the chick say when its mother produced an orange instead of an egg?
"Look at the orange mama laid!"

What happened to the survivors of a collision between a red boat and a blue boat?
They were marooned.

What do you get when a cat eats a lemon?
A sour puss.

What do you call the jester who loses his job?
Nobody's fool.

The Animal Kingdom

"Watch out!" cried the terrified skunk to his pal. "There's a hunter with a gun, and he's headed right toward us!"

The other skunk calmly bowed his head and said, "Let us spray."

•

When Noah opened the door of the ark, he told the animals they could leave, and said, "Now go forth and multiply." All the animals exited the ark except for two snakes coiled together in a far corner.

Noah went over and asked, "Why aren't you going forth and multiplying like all the others?"

"We can't," the snakes replied. "We're adders."

•

The zookeeper spotted a visitor throwing ten-dollar bills into the lions' enclosure. "Hey, mister," he yelled, "why are you doing that?"

The visitor said, "Because the sign says it's okay."

"No, it doesn't," the keeper said.

"Yes, it does," the visitor replied.

"Look: 'Do not feed. $10 fine.'"

Not The Brightest Bulb

"What's the quickest way to downtown
Boston?" asked a visitor as he checked into
a suburban hotel.
"Are you walking or driving?"
"Driving."
"For sure, that's the quickest way."

●

The dim-witted guy went to the store
and bought an AM radio. It took him a month
to realize he could play it at night.

●

In the woods, three novice hunters spotted a set
of tracks. "Hey, deer tracks!" shouted the first.
"No, these are coyote tracks," declared the
second. "You're both wrong," claimed the third.
"These are squirrel tracks if I've ever seen 'em."
They were still arguing when the train came.

You might be as old as Methuselah if...

Your knees go out more often than you do.

You can remember when everything was fields.

You bend down to fasten your shoes and wonder what else you can do while you're down there.

A game of chess leaves you winded.

You remember when the Dead Sea was only sick.

Everything hurts, and what doesn't hurt, doesn't work.

Your kids begin to look middle-aged.

Elevator music brings back fond memories.

Speed limit signs no longer pose a challenge; in fact, you wonder why they let people drive so fast.

Incredible!

A young violinist was auditioning for a seat in an out-of-town orchestra. When the audition ended, the violinist chatted a bit with the conductor. "What do you think of Brahms?" the conductor asked the musician.

"Oh, I absolutely love Brahms!" she enthused. "In fact, he and I were playing duets together just last week."

"And what about Mozart?" queried the conductor. "He's a gem," the violinist gushed. "He really had some great advice for me when we had dinner together last month." Then she looked at her watch and said, "I've got to go now. I don't want to miss the two o'clock train back to Boston."

Later, when the conductor was discussing her audition with members of the orchestra, he said, "Her playing is superb. I feel uneasy about hiring her, though, because I think there's a serious credibility gap. I'm absolutely certain there's no two o'clock train from here to Boston."

The Camping Trip

Mom and Dad wanted to take their two young city-bred sons on their first camping trip in the woods. So they packed the family car and headed off to the mountains. They brought along two tents, one for them and one for the kids.

After everyone was tucked in for the night, mosquitoes came out in force. The boys pulled their blankets over their heads to keep from getting bitten. Soon the younger boy spotted a lightning bug flitting around. "We might as well give up," he said to his brother. "Now they're coming after us with flashlights!"

"Well, my daughter thinks I'm the worst snoop
in the world. At least that's what she wrote
in her diary yesterday."

IT'S TRUE...

You always hear about disgruntled employees,
but never about the gruntled ones.

You can walk into a room nonchalantly,
but not chalantly.

The naughty kids in class are unruly,
but the obedient ones aren't described as ruly.

You might emerge from an accident unscathed,
but if wounded, you aren't scathed.

The carelessly attired individual is disheveled,
but the neatnik isn't heveled, is he?

All God's Children

In Sunday school, the teacher told the children about how Moses led the Children of Israel out of Egypt and across the Red Sea. She explained that they wandered through the desert for forty years, and then entered the Promised Land. At the end of class, one girl stayed behind with a puzzled look on her face.

"What's the matter, Dora?" the teacher asked.

"It's about the Children of Israel, Miss Jones," said Dora. "They left Egypt, crossed the Red Sea, wandered for forty years in the desert and then came to the Promised Land."

"Yes, that's what happened," said the teacher.

"Well, what I want to know is, where were the adults all this time?"

Aren't You Lion?

A young missionary ventured into the African bush to preach the Gospel to villagers in far-flung settlements. One day, walking to an outlying community, a lion started to chase him. The faster he ran, the faster the lion ran! In short order, the missionary found himself trapped by the king of the jungle.

Terrorized and in despair, the missionary fell to his knees and prayed for deliverance. When he opened his eyes, however, he was amazed to discover that the lion, too, was kneeling in prayer. "What a miracle!" exclaimed the man. "You, a killer lion, are joining me in prayer just as I thought my life was going to end!"

The lion looked up. "Shhh," he said, "I'm saying grace."

Doctor, Doctor

The physician examined his patient and then told
him, "You've got plenty of good years left!
Simply eat sensibly, get regular exercise,
and stay away from natural causes."

•

After examining his patient, the doctor said,
"I'm concerned. The skin ointment that I prescribed
for you last month hasn't been doing the job.
You've been using it, haven't you?"
"No, doctor," the patient said. "The directions
say 'apply locally,' and I've been out of town on
business for the past four weeks."

•

The doctor instructed his patient: "Take a pill every
day and walk a mile every day. Call me at the end
of the month. At the end of the month, the patient
called the doctor and cried, "Doc, what do I do
now? I'm thirty miles from home and out of pills!"

•

After the surgeon had operated, the patient
discovered that she had left a sponge in him.
It didn't cause the patient any pain, but he had a
tendency to get really thirsty.

Silly Sayings

What goes around...
gets really dizzy.

The early bird gets the worm...
but the second mouse gets the cheese.

When life hands you lemons...
declare them as a loss on your income tax.

Two wrongs...are only the beginning.

It's never so bad...that it can't get worse.

Strike while...the bug is standing still.

He who hesitates...is probably wise.

If you can't stand the heat...go swimming.

All in Good Taste

As he finished dinner, her husband exclaimed,
"Honey, that was a delicious meal!"
"Thanks," she said. "I thawed it myself."

●

When Mom returned from the grocery store, her young
son grabbed a box of animal crackers that she had
bought. He went to the kitchen table, opened the package, and spread out all the animal-shaped crackers
across the kitchen table. Then he began to study each
one. "What are you doing?" Mom asked.
"It says on the box not to eat them if the seal is
broken," the boy replied, "so I'm looking for the seal."

●

"Prices have really gone up lately," a woman said to
her girlfriend over coffee. "The last time I ate out and
ordered a $30 steak, I told them to put it on my credit
card. And you know what? It fit."

●

A woman went to the meat counter in her local market
and asked the butcher for an ox tail. The butcher said,
"Certainly, ma'am. Once upon a time there was an
ox…"

Buzz, Buzz

An expert on insects who specialized in wasps wandered into an antique shop that carried a selection of old vinyl LPs. Flipping through them, he came across one titled, "Wasps of the World and the Sounds They Make." Intrigued, he asked the sales assistant if he could listen to a few tracks. "Of course," the assistant said. She gave him a headset and sat him down next to an old record player. She pulled the album out of the dust jacket and put it on the turn table.

The wasp expert listened for a few minutes. Then he took off the headphones and announced, "I've researched wasps the world over, and I have never heard any of these sounds from any wasps I've studied!"

"I'm so sorry, sir," the assistant said. "Here, let's try another track." So once again the expert donned the headphones and listened.

"I don't understand it!" he exclaimed after hearing the track through. "I've researched wasps the world over, and I have never heard any of these sounds from any wasps I've studied!"

Yet again the assistant skipped to another track and the man listened. With great agitation, he exclaimed again, quite loudly: "I've researched wasps the world over, and I have never heard any of these sounds from any wasps I've studied!"

Flustered, the assistant picked up the LP and examined it. "Oh, I apologize, sir!" she said, "I just realized I've had this on the bee side!"

All in the Family

Bill thought of a clever way to remember his wife's birthday and their wedding anniversary. He signed up with a flower shop and told them to send flowers to his wife on these dates, along with a note saying, "I love you! Bill." His wife was thrilled to receive the flowers. All went smoothly until one anniversary. Bill arrived home, kissed his wife, and saw the bouquet.
"Nice flowers," he said. "Who from?"

•

A man was buying a fountain pen as a gift. As the clerk wrapped the item, he said, "I imagine this is going to be a surprise, sir." "It certainly is," the customer replied. "It's my son's birthday, and he asked for a new car."

•

One day a little girl looked out the window and saw the neighborhood boys playing a ballgame in the field across the street. She asked, "Grandma, can I go out and play with the boys?" "Oh no, dear," Grandma replied, "they're way too rough." The girl looked out the window again, then said: "Grandma, if I can spot a smooth one, can I play with him?"

WHAT DO YOU CALL...

A snake that drinks too much coffee?
A hyper viper!

A horse that plays the violin?
Fiddler on the hoof!

A cow that cuts grass?
A lawn mooer!

An overweight housecat?
A flabby tabby!

An American's drawing?
A Yankee doodle!

Two spiders who just got married?
Newlywebs!

What do you call a penguin in the Sahara Desert?
Really, really lost!

A man with a kilt on his head?
Scott.

A woman wearing denim?
Jean.

Taste of Heaven

One day, a cat and a mouse died and went to heaven. When they met St. Peter at the Pearly Gates, he asked the mouse what he would like to have for eternity. "I've spent my whole life running from this cat," the mouse said, "so I'd like to have a pair of in-line skates."

"Granted," Peter replied, and immediately the mouse was equipped with skates and he sped off into heaven. Then the saint put the same question to the cat.

"I'd like a nice, soft, fluffy pillow," the cat said, and immediately he found himself lying on the most luxurious pillow he had ever known.

A week later St. Peter saw the cat and inquired how he was doing. "This is wonderful!" the cat purred. "And I especially enjoy your Meals on Wheels!"

Quick Quips

It's not what we possess, but what we enjoy,
that constitutes our abundance.

Science opens to us the book of nature;
comedy, the book of human nature.

There's hope for anyone who can look in the
mirror and laugh at what he sees.

People who agree on what's funny usually agree
on a lot of other things, as well.

For daily happiness, learn to enjoy the scenery
even on a detour.

Enjoy yourself, because these are the "good old days"
you're going to reminisce about later.

A joke that has to be explained is a joke that's
at its wit's end.

"The good news is that you have
a lot of liquid assets.
The bad news is that they've
all gone down the drain."

At Church

As the pastor greeted his parishioners one Sunday
after service, he shook old Walt's hand warmly.
"Brother Walt," he said, "I want you to join the army
of the Lord!"
"Pastor, I'm already in the army of the Lord," Walt
declared.
"Then how come I see you in church only two or three
times a year?"
Walt leaned close to the pastor. "That's because I'm in
the secret service."

●

"Mom," a boy announced one Sunday afternoon,
"I'm going to be a preacher when I grow up!"
"Wonderful," his mother exclaimed. Hoping for a mem-
orable testimony, she asked, "What made you decide to
become a preacher?"
"Well, I have to go to church every Sunday anyhow, and
I figure it'd be more fun to stand up and yell than to sit
down and listen."

●

Walking out of church one Sunday, little Joey looked up
at his grandmother and said, "Grandma, I think you're
just like God." The woman glowed with pleasure,
and wishing to hear more, she said, "And why do you
think that, Joey?" The boy replied: "Because you're both
very, very old."

Favorite hymns for...

Geologists: "Rock of Ages"

Meteorologists: "There Shall Be Showers of Blessings"

Dentists: "Crown Him with Many Crowns"

Construction workers: "A Mighty Fortress Is Our God"

Jet pilots: "I'll Fly Away"

Optometrists: "Be Thou My Vision"

CPAs: "The Old Account Was Settled Long Ago"

Farmers: "We Plough the Fields and Scatter"

All Creatures Great and Small

A boy asked his dad for a pet spider for his birthday. So Dad went to a pet store and asked how much it would cost to buy a spider.

"Fifty dollars," said the clerk.

"Fifty dollars!" exclaimed Dad. "Why, I can get one cheaper on the web!"

•

On the front door of his country inn, the manager posted a sign reading: "Danger! Beware of Dog!" One day as a guest was checking in, he noticed a small, old, harmless-looking pooch snoozing on the floor in front of the desk.

"Is that the dog I'm supposed to beware of?" the guest asked.

"Sure is," said the manager.

The visitor smiled and remarked, "That certainly doesn't look like a dangerous dog to me. I'm curious why you posted that sign."

"Because," the manager explained, "before I put it up, people kept tripping over him."

While a family was walking to church, the daughter was worried she would be late for Sunday school. Her parents gave her permission to run on ahead, and so she did, praying as she ran, "Dear Lord, please don't let me be late! Dear Lord, please don't let me be late!"

Suddenly the girl tripped on a curb and took a tumble, scuffing her shoes, getting her dress dirty, and scraping her hands. She got up, brushed herself off, and started running once again, praying as she ran, "Dear Lord, please don't let me be late! But please don't push me again, either!"

•

Every Sunday, Pastor Jones noticed that one parishioner, Joe, always slipped into the last pew twenty minutes late. Then one Sunday the pastor was astonished to see Joe appear only five minutes past time. Upon greeting the man at the end of the service, the pastor exclaimed, "Good to see you, Joe—this is the earliest you've ever been late!"

How to Pray

Three pastors were having a discussion about the best way to pray while a telephone repairman worked nearby. "Kneeling is the best way to pray," the first pastor said.

"Not really," the second asserted. "One should stand upright with arms upraised to heaven. That's the best way to pray."

"You're both wrong," the third pastor claimed with confidence. "The best way to pray is to lie down with your face to the floor."

Hearing all this, the repairman spoke up. "The best praying I've ever done in my life," he said, "was the time I was hanging upside down from a telephone pole."

How come...

Boxing rings are square?

All those drinks that are supposed to quench your thirst in one gulp come in sixty-four ounce jugs?

Glue never sticks to the inside of the bottle?

We say "after dark" when what we mean is "after light"?

Abbreviated is such a long word?

Bleachers are called "stands" when they're meant for sitting on?

We press harder on the buttons of a remote control when we know the batteries are dead?

When you transport something by car, it's called a shipment; but when you send it by ship, it's called cargo?

Sheep don't shrink when it rains?

WHOSE JOB?

A husband and wife were arguing about who should make the coffee in the morning. She said, "Honey, you should do it because you get up first in the morning."

"No, you should take care of it," he replied, "because you know where things are in the kitchen, and I don't mind waiting."

Annoyed, the wife countered: "You do just fine in the kitchen. Besides, it says in the Bible that the man should make coffee."

"What?" he laughed. "I've never heard of such a thing! You're going to have to show me exactly where the Bible says a man should make coffee."

Without saying anything, she fetched the family Bible, opened it, and pointed to one word on the top of several pages: Hebrews.

Observations

It's not really a small world, after all,
especially if you go everyplace on foot.

A clean house is a sign of a broken computer.

A sure-fire way to forget all your troubles is to
wear tight shoes all day.

To make sure other people take your advice,
find out what they want to do, and then tell
them to do it.

No matter how far you push the envelope,
it will still be stationery.

Don't buy "as-is" parachutes and life preservers.

The only thing you get that's free of charge
is a dead battery.

The great thing about living in a close-knit
community is that if you don't know what
you're doing, someone else does.

Speak On...and On

A corporate vice president was scheduled to speak at a luncheon, so he asked his public relations officer to fire off an upbeat, lighthearted twenty-minute speech. When he returned from the event, he was livid.

"What's the big idea of giving me an hour-long speech?" he shouted. "People were looking at the clock before I was even halfway through!"
The PR officer was astonished. "What do you mean?" he replied. "I did write you a twenty-minute speech, and then I gave you the two copies you requested."

•

The new pastor noticed that committee meetings held by the elders of the congregation often lasted well into the night. He decided to do something about the situation, so he put a notice on the bulletin board one Sunday: "Pastor is leading a workshop titled 'How to Hold One-Hour Meetings.'
The session will take place next Wednesday, 7 - 8:45 p.m.

Only in the Twenty-First Century

A young fellow told his pal that he had asked his sweetheart to marry him. "What did she say?" his pal said. "I don't know," the wooer replied. "She hasn't texted me back yet."

●

A man came home complaining about the day. "Computers were down all afternoon!" he whined, "and I had to do everything manually—even shuffle the deck for solitaire!"

●

The tech support specialist told her caller to right-click. The customer said, "Okay." Then the specialist asked if a pop-up window appeared. When the customer said "no," the specialist said, "Please right-click again, then." When the customer reported no pop-up window, the specialist said, "Okay, I want you to tell me exactly what you have done up to this point."
The customer said, "Sure. You told me to write 'click,' and so I wrote 'click.'"

●

The teenager was growing frustrated as he tried to show his dad how to program the remote control. Finally he sighed, "You know, this would be a lot easier if you were 12."

Healthy Living

An elderly couple died on the same day and arrived together at the Pearly Gates. St. Peter offered to show them around. He led the couple along streets paved with gold. Spacious homes were surrounded by lush parks, rolling golf courses, sparkling lakes, and rippling streams filled with fish. At last they came to the couple's eternal abode, a beautiful home equipped with the latest electronics, plus a shiny new sports car parked in the garage.

"Darn it, Margie," the husband said as soon as St. Peter left them, "we could have had all this twenty years earlier if you hadn't insisted we start that stupid diet and exercise program!"

•

A woman wanted to lose weight, so she asked her doctor about a diet. "I want you to eat regularly for two days, and then skip one day," he advised. "Repeat the procedure for a month, and you're sure to lose five pounds."

When the woman returned after a month, the doctor was amazed to discover that she had lost not five pounds, but twenty pounds. "That's wonderful!" he exclaimed. "You must have followed my advice!"

"I sure did," the woman said, "but I nearly dropped on that third day."
"From hunger?"
"No," she said, "from skipping."

The Mouths of Babes

One day when Dad was driving with his young daughter, he honked his horn by mistake. "I did that by accident," he told her.

"Yes, I know that, Daddy," she said.

"How do you know that?" he asked, pleased with his daughter's perception.

"Easy," she said. "You didn't lower the window and holler at the other driver after you honked."

•

When the Millers moved into their larger home, little Brian was telling Grandma about the new place.

"It's really great," he said. "Meg has her own room, the twins have their own room, and I have my own room." Then he lowered his voice and confided, "It's too bad, though, because Mom and Dad still have to share theirs."

•

A little boy went to the library and wanted to check out a book called A Guide for Mothers. "Are you getting this for your mother?" the librarian asked as he handed her the book.

"No, ma'am," he said, "it's for me. I want to start collecting moths."

Signs you've had too much coffee...

You walk 20 miles on your treadmill before you discover it's not plugged in.

You grind coffee beans in your mouth.

You ski uphill.

You short out motion detectors.

You help your dog chase its tail.

You can type 70 words a minute…with your feet.

You believe being referred to as a "drip" is a compliment.

You answer the door before people knock.

You speed walk in your sleep.

WIT AND WISDOM

Often the truth spoken with a smile will penetrate the mind and reach the heart; the lesson strikes home without wounding because of the wit in the saying.

Horace

•

Wrinkles should merely indicate
where smiles have been.

Mark Twain

•

Mirth is God's medicine. Everybody ought to bathe in it. Grim care, moroseness, anxiety—all this rust of life— ought to be scoured off by the oil of mirth.

Henry Ward Beecher

•

Humor brings insight and tolerance.

Agnes Repplier

•

A good laugh is sunshine in a house.

William Makepeace Thackeray

Top Speed

A curious fellow had a question. He wanted to know how fast his racing bicycle could go before it became uncontrollable. To answer his question, he asked a buddy who owned a flashy sports car if he could tie his bike to the back of his car. That way he could easily discover the bicycle's top speed. "Sure," his buddy said.

So the fellow tied his bike to the back of the sports car. He said to his buddy, "I'll ring my bike bell once if I want you to go faster, twice if I want you to maintain speed, and repeatedly if I want you to slow down."

With that, off they went. In the beginning, things went very well. As the driver increased speed, the bicycle performed admirably, and the cyclist was thrilled. But as the car reached speeds over 60 m.p.h., an even flashier sports car pulled up beside the driver. Sensing a challenge, the cyclist's driver put the pedal to the metal and the two sports cars began drag racing. The fellow on the bicycle quickly realized he had reached the limit of his ride's endurance.

At the crossroads sat a state trooper in his cruiser, radar gun in hand. The cars whizzed by him and his radar gun flashed 110 m.p.h. Too astonished to chase the speeders, he called in to the dispatcher.

"No one's going to believe this," he said, "but two revved up sports cars are drag racing out here on the highway, and there's a guy behind them on a bike ringing his bell like mad trying to pass them!"

Maybe you're spending too much time on your computer if...

You automatically add ".com" after your home address.

Your spouse sends you an email telling you that dinner is ready.

You decline into depression when there's no new mail in your inbox.

Your computer and all its accessories cost more than your car.

You'll eat at restaurants with bad food if they have free Internet access.

You refuse to communicate with relatives who aren't on social media.

You have more friends on the Internet than in real life.

Q&A TIME: SPORTS

Who is the world's fastest runner?
Adam. He was the first in the human race.

What did the athlete on the trampoline say?
"Life has its ups and downs, but I always bounce back."

Why couldn't the tennis player figure out how to boil water?
Because she had lost all her matches.

What did the soccer ball say to the soccer player?
"I get a kick out of you!"

Why did the golfer wear two pairs of pants?
In case he got a hole in one.

What is the hardest thing about learning to ice skate?
The ice.

Why did the martial arts teacher call in sick?
Because he had kung flu.

"Funny thing—I keep smelling carrots."

Buyer's Market

Long ago, a sultan found himself deeply in debt. He began to sell his treasures, and at last came to his prized possession, the Star of the Euphrates. The gem was the most valuable diamond in the world.

Reluctantly, he took it to the pawn shop. The pawnbroker examined the diamond and offered him $100,000 for it. "Are you nuts? I paid over $2,000,000 for this!" the sultan screamed. "Do you have any idea who I am?"

The man behind the counter replied, "When you wish to pawn a star, makes no difference who you are."

•

A husband splurged on a motor boat, despite his wife's vehement objection. Hoping to soothe her anger at his extravagance, he promised her that she could name the boat. Being a good sport, she accepted his offer.

When her husband went to the dock to take his prized possession out for a maiden voyage, he saw the vessel's name printed on the side in big red letters: For Sale.

Little Acts of Kindness

The new pastor was walking through the neighborhood when he spied a small boy straining to reach
the doorbell of a house. So the good man quickly
went to the porch and rang the doorbell for him.
"Now what?" he asked the boy.
"Run like crazy!" said the boy,
"because that's what I'm planning to do!"

•

Little Daniel has been misbehaving in church and
was sent to the nursery for a needed time-out. After
church had ended, the pastor came in to talk to him.
"I prayed about it while I was in here,"
the boy explained.
"Excellent!" the pastor said. "If you asked God to help
you behave better in church, He will help you."
"Oh, I didn't pray for that," the boy said. "I asked God
to help you put up with me."

•

A man went to visit his friend in another city.
"Remember last year when I was broke and you
helped me out? I told you at the time that I'd never
forget your generosity."
"Yes, I remember," his friend replied.
"Well, guess what," his visitor said. "I'm broke again."

Pumping Iron

Dad was skeptical about his teenage son's new-found interest in working out. Nonetheless, the two went to the sporting goods store and his son pointed to a set of weights that he had had his eye on. "Please, Dad," the boy said, "I promise I'll use them every day."

"It's a big commitment," his dad warned.

"I know that, Dad," the boy replied.

"And they're certainly not cheap," Dad said as he looked at the price tag.

"I'll really use them," his son said. "Just you wait and see."

Finally won over, Dad paid for the equipment and they turned to leave the store. That's when Dad heard his son say, "You mean I have to carry this all the way to the car?"

Forgive Us Our Trespasses

A professor assigned his seminary students an essay. "I want you to write a two-page paper on one of the seven deadly sins," he said. The next day as students were handing in their assignment, one said to another, "This was so easy. All I did was write a one-page essay and double-space it." "Never thought of that," his classmate said. "Which sin did you pick?" "Sloth."

●

An elderly woman wanted to mail the family Bible to her daughter in another state. When she put the package on the post office counter, the clerk asked, "Is there anything breakable in here?" "Only the Ten Commandments," the woman replied with a smile.

●

Jim's wife was worried about her husband playing golf on Sundays. She searched through the Bible for a verse on the subject, but found nothing. Finally she went to her pastor and asked, "Is it okay for Jim to play golf on Sundays?" "Well, the Commandments would say it's a sin," the cleric said, "and knowing the way he plays, it's also a crime."

HAVE YOU EVER NOTICED THAT...

Bacon fat splatters all over the kitchen when you fry it; but the fat gathers all in one place when you eat it?

Low-fat bread tastes a whole lot better when its slathered with butter and cream cheese?

A grapefruit always seems to know where your eye is?

The more expensive the meal, the smaller the portions?

When you hang something in your closet for two months, it shrinks two sizes?

You can order a club sandwich even if you're not a member?

In Uniform

One morning, the drill sergeant stood in front of a group of new recruits. "Today I have some good news and some bad news," he declared. "The good news is that Private Thomas will be setting the pace on our morning run."

The soldiers cheered, as Private Thomas was neither athletic nor energetic. The sergeant continued: "The bad news is that Private Thomas will be driving a truck."

●

The sergeant-major fixed his eyes on the new recruit. "Soldier!" he growled, "I didn't see you at camouflage training this morning!"

"Thank you, sir."

●

Three servicemen were bragging about the deeds of their ancestors. The first declared, "My great-granddad was a drummer boy at Shiloh." The second reported that his great-granddad fought alongside Custer at the Battle of the Little Big Horn. The third hung his head and shuffled his feet. "I'm the only soldier in my family," he confessed, "but if my great-granddad were still alive today, he'd be famous all over the world." "How come?" asked his companions. "Because he'd be 177 years old."

Hard to Please

Max was walking down the street looking down-cast. "Why so glum, guy?" asked a friend.

"Let me tell you," Max said. "Three weeks ago, an elderly aunt passed away and left me $10,000."

"Well, I'm certainly sorry to hear about your aunt," the friend said. "But how good of her to leave you a little change, huh?"

"That's not all," Max continued. "Two weeks ago, I got a tax refund of $25,000 that I didn't expect."

"Wow, that's fantastic!" raved his friend.

"Then last week I won $50,000 in a contest I entered," Max said, still looking glum.

"That's absolutely fabulous!" his friend said. "Why in the world are you looking so unhappy?"

Max stopped and looked at his friend. "Because this week…nothing."

HOUSEHOLD HINTS... FOR THE UNINSPIRED

1. Cobwebs are spiders' homes. Don't contribute to the problem of homeless spiders by taking down their webs.

2. Dust bunnies make wonderful, easy-to-care for pets. Besides, they get bigger even if you don't feed them anything.

3. Wet-mopped floors increase the chance of someone slipping on them. Avoid a trip to the emergency room by not mopping.

4. Vacuuming uses electricity. Save on your utility bills by not vacuuming.

5. Birds fly into clear, sparkling windows. Be kind to birds by maintaining dirty panes.

6. When things are out, you can easily locate them. Never put your possessions in drawers and closets.

7. The best way to keep a clean kitchen is not to cook in it. Eat out tonight.

8. Follow reason #7, and you won't need to wash dishes, either. There won't be any.

9. If you dust, you'll get the duster dirty. Why transfer dust from one place to another?

10. Housework is one of those things no one notices until you don't do it. So give your friends and family something to notice!

It's Raining Cats and Dogs

Nothing in the world is friendlier than a wet dog,
or a cat with tuna on her breath.

Dogs have owners; cats have staff.

To catch a runaway dog, call his name and he'll
come running into your arms.

To catch a runaway cat, ignore her and she'll
saunter up to you when she's good and ready.

To the cat, every human is a food dispenser—
which explains why cats put up with humans.

You can teach a dog any trick you want him to do.
Your cat will teach you any trick she wants you to do.

Bring a new dog home, and you can train him.
Bring a new cat home, and she will train you.

WHY?

Dad was shooting baskets in the park with his young son when the boy asked, "Dad, why are we here?"

Delighted for the opening to impart some of his fatherly wisdom, Dad launched into a lengthy discourse on what is important in life. "Son, we're not here to live for ourselves alone, or to make money, or to chase after fame," Dad finally concluded. "We're here to be of use in the world, take responsibility, to give back, to be the best we can be. Does that help?"

The boy shook his head and said, "No, not really."

Puzzled, Dad asked, "Well, what's still bothering you?"

"I was just wondering why we're here when Mom asked us to pick her up from the store an hour ago."

"But we've *got* to have raisins, Grandma!
How else are they going to be able to see?"

Quick Quips

A smile is a passport that will take you anywhere
you want to go.

Shoot for the moon. Even if you miss it,
you'll land among the stars.

What soap is to the body, laughter is to the soul.

When you get to the end of your rope,
tie a knot and hang on.

Don't be afraid to try something new.
Remember, amateurs built Noah's ark;
professionals built the Titanic.

Even if there's nothing to laugh about,
laugh on credit.

With each sunrise, we start anew.

Enjoy the little things—there are so many of them.

GETTING A JOB

An interviewer asked an applicant whether he had any unusual talents to offer the company. He announced proudly that he had won several prizes in crossword puzzle competitions, slogan-writing contests, and on-line interactive games. "Fine," said the interviewer, "but we're looking for someone who can be smart during office hours." "Oh," replied the applicant, "all that was during office hours!"

•

A hiring manager of a department store was looking at a potential employee's application. She noticed that the man had never worked in retail before. She said, "For someone with no prior experience, your salary expectations are high."
"Well," replied the applicant, "that's because the work is so much harder when you don't know what you're doing."

•

The interviewer said to the young man, "For this job, we're looking for someone who's responsible."
"I'm the right person!" the applicant said happily. "In my last job, whenever something went wrong, they found me responsible!"

DOCTOR, DOCTOR

An obstetrician had worked her way through medical school while working part-time at the grocery deli counter. This became apparent the first time she delivered a baby, held it up for the mother to see, and said, "A little over seven pounds. Is that okay?"

•

After a thorough examination, the doctor said to his patient, "I'm afraid your health isn't good at all. The best thing for you to do is start exercising an hour a day. Stop eating fatty foods, drinking sugary sodas, snacking on potato chips, and munching on candy bars. And give up the late-night shows so you can get at least eight hours of sleep every night."

The patient listened and then said, "So, doc, what's the next best thing?"

•

"Doctor," the patient said, "will I be able to play the piano after my surgery?"

"Certainly," the doctor assured the patient, "you should be able to play it with ease."

"Great!" said the patient. "You know, I could never play it before."

If...

The grass is greener on your neighbor's side
of the fence, console yourself by remembering
that his water bill is much higher than yours.

Trains stop at train stations and buses stop at
bus stations, what happens at work stations?

You think things can't get any worse,
you're just not thinking hard enough.

The black box flight recorder can withstand
a crash, why don't they make the whole plane
out of the same stuff?

You haven't gotten all the things you want,
be grateful for the things you didn't get that
you don't want.

You try to fail and succeed, have you failed
or succeeded?

Elbows bent the other way, what would
saxophones look like?

If golf had never been invented, how would
we measure hail?

On the Road

As he was driving between two small rural towns, the man's car stalled. When he got out of the vehicle and opened the hood to find out what was the matter, a cow sauntered over and stood beside him for a few minutes. "Problem is with the fuel line," the cow said, and then continued her stroll down the road.

The man was flabbergasted. He watched wide-eyed as the cow lumbered out of sight. In a few minutes, a farmer came along on his tractor, stopped, and hopped down. "Can I help ya'?" he asked. In a trembling voice, the man told the farmer what had happened.

"Hmmm," said the farmer. "Was that a large red cow with a brown spot over her right eye?"

"Yes, yes," the man replied excitedly. "That's the one!"

"I wouldn't listen to her," the farmer said. "Ol' Bessie doesn't know a thing about car engines."

Ooops!

Doris planned a cross-country vacation, staying at various friends' and relatives' houses along the way. Her first stop was the home of Aunt Lorie who was organized to the nth degree. Knowing this, Doris said to her aunt on the first day of her stay: "Aunt Lorie, you'll be impressed to know that I've already written thank-you notes to everyone I'll be staying with during my entire trip!"

"Oh," replied the aunt hesitantly. "That wouldn't be that little stack of envelopes I put in the mail for you this morning, would it?"

•

A little boy knocked on his neighbor's door. When she answered it, he said, "Mrs. Taylor, there's something of mine in your garage, and I'd like to get it back."

Perplexed, Mrs. Taylor opened her garage door and discovered a baseball on the floor and a baseball-size hole in the window.

"Now how do you suppose that ball got in here?" she said sternly.

"Dunno," the boy said. "But I guess it could have come in through the hole in the window."

Q&A Time: Food

How come the farmer ploughed his field with a steam roller?
Because he wanted to grow mashed potatoes.

How do you make an egg roll?
Easy—push it downhill.

What did the toast say to the bread?
Pop up and see me sometime.

How does a casserole acquire good taste?
A little seasoning will do it.

Where can a hamburger get a good night's sleep?
On a bed of lettuce.

What do you give to a wounded lemon?
Lemon aid.

Why did the cabbage win the race?
Because he was a head.

MONEYWISE

The quickest way to double your money
is to fold it and put it back in your pocket.

Will Rogers

•

With money in your pocket, you are wise,
and you are handsome, and you sing well, too.

Proverb

•

One must be poor to know the luxury of giving.

George Eliot

•

There are two times in a man's life
when he should not speculate:
when he can't afford it, and when he can.

Mark Twain

•

A wise man should have money in his head,
but not in his heart.

Jonathan Swift

The Mouths of Babes

On a field trip, the kindergarten class visited the local hospital. During the tour, a technician showed them X-rays of broken bones. "Have any of you ever broken a bone?" she asked.
"I have," one little girl said.
"Did it hurt?" the technician asked.
"No, it didn't hurt," the girl responded.
"Oh," said the technician, "you must be a very brave little girl! Which bone did you break?"
"My sister's arm."

●

At the end of a family meal at an elegant restaurant, Dad asked the waiter for a box so he could take home the steak bones to his dog. His young son's eyes brightened, and he cried, "Oh, wow, Dad! That means I can finally have a puppy?"

●

A little girl came home from school.
"I got in trouble for something I didn't do!" she said to her mother. "Oh, I'm sorry," replied her mother sympathetically. "I'll have a talk with your teacher. What was it that you didn't do?"
"My homework."

Silly Sayings

A penny saved is...
not worth too much anymore.

When it rains...
it's time to get out your umbrella.

An idle mind...
is the best way to relax.

The shortest distance between two points...
is usually under construction.

Early to bed, early to rise...
means you're bored with late-night TV.

Better safe than...
pick a fight with someone.

Look before you...
trip over something.

A miss is as good as...
a mister.

Where there's smoke, there's...
pollution.

Wacky Definitions

Birth of twins.....
an infant replay.

Acorn...
an oak in a nutshell.

A chicken crossing the road...
poultry in motion.

Hamlet...
a tiny pig.

Procrastination...
the art of keeping up with yesterday.

Acupuncture...
a jab well done.

Pillow...
a nap sack.

Compliment...
applause that refreshes.

Lamb...
an animal that gets more sheepish with age.

"I thought the first one was."

Country Road

Highway maintenance workers were sent out to replace road signs that had been knocked over in a fierce storm the week before. The first downed sign they came to was a symbol warning of a deer crossing. They tossed the damaged sign into their truck and put up a new one. As they moved on down the road, one worker happened to look back and noticed that two deer were running across the road. He turned to his co-worker, pointed to the deer, and said, "Makes me wonder how long they've been waiting to cross."

●

A man was walking along a country road when he spotted a farmer working in his field. "Hello," the man called to the farmer. "How long will it take me to get to town?"

The farmer didn't answer. After the man waited a few minutes, he shrugged his shoulders and resumed walking. Then he heard the farmer yell out, "About twenty minutes."

"Thanks," the man shouted back, "but how come you didn't tell me when I first asked you?"

"'Cause I had no idea how fast you could walk."

Books and More Books

Hear about...

The writer who wrote a best-seller?
The only thing missing were best-buyers.

The reader who asked the librarian for tips on how to read faster?
She suggested he quit coloring the pictures.

The customer who bought a book called "How to Handle Disappointment"?
When he got the book home, all the pages were blank.

The cat who swallowed a skein of yarn?
She had mittens.

The bookstore customer who asked where the self-help section was located?
The clerk said, "No way! That would defeat the whole purpose!"

The greatest American novel?
It's the one no one has read, but everyone talks about.

Class Act

A history teacher was quizzing her students on the British kings and queens that they had studied the previous day. "Who followed Edward VI?" she asked.

"Mary," said a girl at the back of the class.

"Right!" said the teacher. "And then who followed Mary?"

"Her little lamb," the girl answered.

•

The third-grade class went on a field trip to the community fire house. After an interesting and informative tour, the fire chief asked each student something about fire safety. He pointed to Kyle and said, "Now what would you do if your clothes caught fire?"

He replied promptly, "I sure wouldn't put them on!"

The Mouths of Babes

The husband and wife, new members of the
congregation, joined their church-family at the
Sunday afternoon potluck. Near the end of the
meal, the wife nudged her husband. "You've had
four desserts!" she hissed. "The woman at the
dessert table is going to think you're a glutton!"
"No she won't," her husband said between
mouthfuls of apple pie. "I told her that
the desserts were for you!"

•

Carl had a leak in the ceiling over his dining room,
so he called a repairman to fix it.
"When did you discover the leak?"
the repairman asked.
"Yesterday, when it took me two hours
to finish my soup," Carl replied.

•

A young woman and her boyfriend had been dating
for quite a while, and she was eager to start talking
about marriage. Nothing happened, however, after
still more time together. Then one evening the two
went to a Chinese restaurant. Scanning the menu,
the boyfriend casually asked her, "So, how do you
like your rice? Steamed or fried?"
She looked at him and said, "Thrown."

Home Sweet Home

A homeowner received a strongly worded "second notice" that his house payment was overdue. In a panic, he rushed to the mortgage company and paid his bill, all the while apologizing to the clerk that he apparently had lost or overlooked the first notice.

"Oh," the clerk said, "don't worry about it, because we don't send out first notices. We've found that second notices are much more effective."

•

The homeowner, an elderly gent, was sitting on his front porch one afternoon when a young fellow walked up with a pad and pencil in his hand.

"What are you selling?" the homeowner asked.

"I'm not selling anything, sir," the fellow replied. "I'm a census taker."

"A what?" the homeowner said.

"A census taker. We're trying to find out how many people are in the United States."

"You're wasting your time with me," the homeowner declared, "because I have no idea."

Worth a Second Look

CORRECTION: The recipe for One-Egg Cake in the church cookbook was written as needing two eggs. It actually needs three eggs.

FOR LEASE: 1-2 bdrm apartments. No poets.

HELP WANTED: Five yrs work experience required. Men or women only.

SPECIAL OF THE DAY: Bacon, lettuce, and tomato sandwiches made with bacon, lettuce, and tomato.

FOR SALE: Two-carat embezzled diamond ring. Gorgeous.

HOMES TOUR: Visit open houses in our town's hysterical district on Sunday, 1-4.

NOTICE: The fitness class will meet for an all-you-can-eat pancake breakfast Saturday morning.

WANTED: Would like to trade a 9 x 13 casserole dish for a 13 x 9 casserole dish.

The Lumberjack

A logging company put out a call for a good lumberjack. The next morning, a scrawny-looking fellow carrying an ax strode into the camp and rapped on the headman's door. The headman gave him the once-over, then promptly asked him to leave and not waste his time.

"Give me a chance," pleaded the man. "Let me show you what I can do."

"Okay, little guy," the headman said gruffly. "See that giant oak over there? Go chop it down."

The scrawny man walked over to the tree. Five minutes later he was back in the headman's office and pointed to a stack of oak wood piled where the tree had stood. "Done," he said.

The headman was astonished. "Where'd you get the know-how to do something like that?" he asked.

"In the Sahara Forest," the scrawny man said proudly.

"You mean the Sahara Desert," said the headman.

"No, sir," the man said. "*Now* they call it the Sahara Desert!"

Quick Quips

Knowledge is when you know that the street is a one-way street. Wisdom is looking both ways anyway.

The one great thing about egomaniacs is that they don't talk about other people.

As long as there are algebra tests, there will be prayer in school.

Nothing needs reforming as much as other people's habits.

Push will get you anywhere—except through doors marked "Pull."

Anyone who says "I slept like a baby" has never actually had a baby.

We start cutting our wisdom teeth the first time we bite off more than we can chew.

Doggone It!

A woman saw a sign in a pet shop: "Talking Dog for Sale - $10." Curious, she stepped inside and asked to see the talking dog. The store owner brought out a rather ordinary looking mutt. "Can you talk?" the woman asked the dog.

"Sure can," the dog replied.

"Then tell me about yourself," she said.

"I found out I could talk when I was just a pup," the dog said. "I love my country, so I offered my services to the CIA, and in no time I was attending top-level meetings in the major capitals of the world. Then I'd report back everything I had heard. I did this for ten years.

"Then I did some undercover work for the police department and foiled not a few criminal plots. But all that got tiring after a while, so now I'm retired."

"Wow," exclaimed the woman to the store owner. "Why in the world are you selling him for only ten dollars?"

"Because he's a liar," the man said. "He hasn't done any of those things!"

BEWARE

A woman's air conditioning unit zonked out in the middle of summer, and she frantically called a repairman. He promised to come the next morning, however, she needed to attend an important business meeting at the same time. So she told him that she'd leave a key under a pot of flowers on the porch, and he could let himself in. She asked him to leave his bill on the counter, and she'd mail a check immediately.

In addition, she told him he'd see a particularly ferocious-looking pit bull, but that the dog wouldn't bother him at all. But she added: "Don't under any circumstances say anything to the parrot. Leave him alone, no matter what!"

The next morning, the repairman arrived, found the key, and entered the woman's home. He discovered the pit bull lying on the floor asleep. Though he looked mean, he didn't even lift his head as the man gingerly stepped around him. He saw the parrot on a perch, who eyed him suspiciously, but didn't make a sound.

As soon as the man started working on the woman's A/C unit, however, the parrot began to yell. The bird knew every insult under the sun and hurled each one several times at the hapless repairman. After an hour of listening to the onslaught, the man lost his temper completely. "Be quiet, you dumb old bird," he screamed, "Quit yelling at me or I'll pull your ugly feathers out!"

A moment's silence ensued, then the parrot said calmly and clearly, "Go sic 'em, Bruiser!"

"He's got a great 10-minute sermon,
but it takes him an hour to give it."

GRACE

In a small town, the Baptist church's pastor was also the town barber. A newcomer to the community visited the shop and sat down for a haircut and shave. The pastor introduced himself and proceeded to cut the man's hair. When the job was done, he said, "Stay here, and my wife, Grace, will take care of the shave." With that, the pastor/barber went on to the next customer.

Grace appeared, and gave him a careful shave while chatting merrily. When she was done, the man asked her what he owed. "Fifteen for the haircut, twenty-five for the shave," she said. Though he thought the price of the shave somewhat high, he went ahead and paid her. After leaving the shop, he decided that once a week for a haircut would be fine, but he wouldn't go there every day for a shave.

The next morning he woke up and stood in front of the mirror. Not a speck of stubble showed, and his face was as smooth as it was right after his shave the previous day. Next morning, the same result. Four days later, his face remained silky smooth. "Well, that was worth twenty-five dollars," he thought to himself.

The following week, the man entered the barber shop again and exclaimed to the pastor how he had not had to shave for the entire week, and his face was still completely stubble-free. "It's a miracle!" the customer said.

The pastor smiled and said gently, "Brother, you were shaved by Grace, and once shaved, always shaved."

Cootchie-Coo

One afternoon a proud papa was taking his infant daughter out for a stroll in the park. When he saw the sparrows flitting in the trees, he leaned down to her buggy and said, "Look! See all the pretty birdies?" As he approached the pond, he said, "Look! See the pretty blue water and all the fishies swimming around?"

As a woman walking her dog approached from the other direction, the man exclaimed excitedly, "Look, sweetie! See the nice little doggy?"

Suddenly he realized how silly he must sound to the woman, talking to an infant as if she could understand every word he said. But just as Papa and buggy passed the dog walker, the woman bent down to her dog and said, "Look! See the darling little baby?"

"She wants to hit the high notes."

Have you heard the one about...

The skunk who realized that the wind had changed? It all started to come back to him.

The book titled, "A Thousand Ways to Avoid Rip-offs"? There are only 500 ideas in it.

The guy who always made a long story short? He kept forgetting the ending.

The golfer who gave up trying to shoot his age on the course. Now he's aiming for his area code.

The dieter who learned she shouldn't have double-fudge brownies for dessert? So now she has them as an appetizer.

The employee who wanted more recognition? The boss told him to wear a name tag.

The guy who ordered a waffle with his alphabet soup? He wanted to do a crossword puzzle.

The fellow who took two months off work so he could finish the novel he was working on? Gives you an idea what a slow reader he was.

Value Added

A humble cobbler had worked in his shop for decades when an upscale restaurant went in beside his small and cramped establishment. Soon delectable aromas were emanating from the restaurant's kitchen, and the cobbler started eating his lunch outside the kitchen so he could enjoy whiffs of fine fare as he ate his baloney sandwich.

After this had gone on for a month, the cobbler received a bill from the restaurant for "enjoyment of food." Puzzled, he went next door to the restaurant and explained to the manager that he had never eaten there, as he could not afford anything on the menu. The manager said, "I've seen you enjoying what comes out of our kitchen at lunchtime, so you should pay for it."

The cobbler refused to pay, and the restaurant manager took him to court. At the hearing, the judge asked the manager to present his complaint. "Every day," he said, "this man comes out of his shop, sits near our kitchen, and smells our expensive food while eating his baloney sandwich. Clearly, we're providing added value to his lunch, and we deserve compensation for it."

The judge turned to the cobbler and asked what he had to say about the situation. The cobbler, however, didn't speak a word in his defense. Instead, he put his hand in his pocket and rattled a few dimes and quarters around.

"What's the meaning of this?" the judge asked.

The cobbler replied, "I'm paying for the smell of his food with the sound of my money."

How come...

Round pies come in square boxes?

We call it "rush hour" when no one can go faster than 5 m.p.h.?

Irons have a permanent press setting?

"Economy-size" means big in detergents and small in cars?

It's always the driver in the third car back that's first to see the light turn green?

There are five syllables in the word "monosyllable"?

Cat hairs seem to stick to everything except the cat?

Open Wide

"Open, please," said the dentist to the patient. After a few minutes, the dentist exclaimed, "My goodness, this is the biggest cavity I've ever seen– the biggest cavity that I've ever seen!"

"Doctor," protested the patient, "I'm scared enough without you saying that twice."

"I didn't," said the dentist. "That was the echo."

●

A woman and her husband had to interrupt their European tour to see a dentist. "I want a tooth pulled," the woman explained, "and I don't want to take time with numbing the gum or anything. Just pull it as fast as possible so we can get back to our tour."

The dentist was surprised. "You're certainly brave," he said. "Now show me which tooth you want pulled."

The woman turned to her husband and said, "Show him the tooth, honey."

Late Again

Mr. Smith, the office manager, called a new employee into his office. He explained to her that her constant tardiness was not acceptable. "Other employees have noticed that you come in the front door fifteen minutes late every morning," he said. She thought about the situation a moment and then said, "So, is there another door I can use?"

•

A clerk had a problem getting up for work in the mornings, and he was frequently reprimanded for being late. He decided to do something about the problem. He went to the doctor, who gave him a pill to take before bedtime. So the clerk followed the doctor's instructions, went to bed, slept soundly, and woke up feeling refreshed. He looked at the clock and was delighted to find that he had time for a leisurely breakfast before he went into work.

"Good morning," he chirped to his boss. "I think all my problems with getting up in the morning are taken care of! I feel great!"

"Wonderful," said his boss. "But where were you yesterday?"

IN THE WAITING ROOM

Bert was sitting in his doctor's waiting room when he heard someone shouting from the examining room, "Measles! Typhoid! Tetanus!" Perplexed, Bert went up to the receptionist and asked what was going on.
"Oh, that's just Dr. Jones," she replied.
"He likes to call the shots around here."

•

A man was sitting in a doctor's waiting room, and he was praying, "Lord, I hope I'm sick! I hope I'm sick!"
After this went on for several minutes, the woman next to him asked, "Sir, I know it's none of my business, but why are you praying that you are sick?"
The man said, "I'd hate to think I'm well and feel the way I do."

•

A physician, dashing through his full waiting room to move his double-parked car, turned to his patients and said, "I'll be back in a minute—don't anyone get well until I return!"

WIT AND WISDOM

Do not judge each day by the harvest you reap
but by the seeds that you plant.
Robert Louis Stevenson

•

The real voyage of discovery consists not in
seeking new landscapes, but in having new eyes.
Marcel Proust

•

If there be no remedy, why worry?
Proverb

•

Be careless in your dress if you must,
but keep a tidy soul.
Mark Twain

•

My way of joking is to tell the truth.
It's the funniest joke in the world.
George Bernard Shaw

The Mouths of Babes

Little Emily came home from school one day complaining of a stomachache. Her mother said, "That's probably because it's empty. You'll feel much better after you have something in it." Sure enough, Emily felt fine after eating the snack her mother fixed for her.

That afternoon the minister dropped in for a visit. While he has chatting with Emily's mom, he mentioned that he'd had a headache all day long. Emily perked up. "That's because it's empty," she said, "and you'd feel better if you had something in it!"

•

The pastor was talking to one of his young parishioners who told him that his mother says a bedtime prayer for him every night. "That's wonderful!" the pastor said. "And what does she say before she turns out the light?"

"Thank God, he's finally going to sleep."

Too True!

A young pastor, fresh out of the seminary, decided that it might help him better understand the temptations, fears, and stresses that his future congregants faced if he worked as a police officer for a year. He passed the physical exam and went on to take the oral exam. The questions tested his ability to act quickly and wisely in tense situations. He was asked: "What would you do to disperse an unruly crowd?"

"Easy," the pastor said. "I'd pass the offering plate."

•

A college freshman walked up to his roommate and said, "I got us a cookbook so we can cook some of our own food. Trouble is, we can't make any of the recipes."

"Why not?" inquired the roommate. "Are they all really complicated?"

"No," the freshman replied. "It's just that they all start out with the same thing: 'Take a clean bowl.'"

QUICK QUIPS

An optimist is a person who, instead of feeling sorry he cannot pay his bills, is glad that he's not one of his creditors.

God gives the nuts, but he does not crack them for us.

The trouble with stretching the truth is that it often snaps back.

The best time to think about retirement is before the boss does.

People who fall for get-rich-quick schemes have been led astray by false profits.

You can't make footprints in the sands of time while you're sitting down.

The best place to put your troubles is in your pocket—the one with a hole in it.

In Sunday School

The week before Christmas, the pre-school Sunday school teacher asked her class, "What was Jesus' mother's name?"

"Mary," answered Lisa.

"Good!" said the teacher. "Now who can tell me Jesus' father's name?"

"Verge," answered Lily.

"Verge," the teacher said, confused. "Where did you get that?"

Lily said, "'Cause Pastor's been talking about Verge 'n' Mary."

•

A Sunday school teacher wanted her class of first graders to memorize the Twenty-third Psalm. Through the following month, each child made good progress except for one. Try as he might, the little boy couldn't get past the first line.
When the time came for the class to recite the Psalm in front of the congregation, she made it easy on the little boy by letting him go first. He stepped forward and said in a loud, strong voice: "The Lord is my Shepherd, and that's all I need to know."

Not the Best Bets

During a long airline flight, a scholar with ency-
clopedic knowledge became intensely bored. He
turned to the sleeping passenger seated next to
him, nudged the man awake, and asked him if he'd
like to play a game.

"I'll ask you a question," the scholar explained.
"If you don't know the answer, you pay me five
dollars. Then you ask me a question, and if I don't
know, I'll pay you fifty dollars." The man agreed. So
the scholar asked: "What's the distance from the
earth to the moon?" Shrugging his shoulders, the
man handed the scholar five dollars. "It's 238,857
miles," the scholar said smugly. "Now you ask me
a question."

The man thought for a moment, then said: "What
goes up a hill with three legs and comes down with
four?"

The scholar was silent for an hour as he tried to
figure out the answer. Finally, he handed the man
fifty dollars. "Okay, tell me what the answer is!" he
cried in exasperation.

"I have no idea," the man said as he pulled out a
five-dollar bill, handed it to the scholar, and promptly went back to sleep.

An archaeologist digging in the Holy Land unearthed a casket containing a mummy. He announced to his colleagues, "I've just found a 3,000-year-old mummy of a man who died of heart failure."

Tests on the mummy proved the man correct. One of his colleagues asked him, "How did you know the man had died of heart failure?"
"Easy," replied the archaeologist. "I found a note on him that said '500,000 shekels on Goliath.'"

●

Several top-winning race horses were staying in a stable near the race track. One started to talk about his track record. "In the last 15 races, I came in first in eight of them," he bragged.

Another horse spoke up. "In the last 27 races, I've won 19!"

"Nice, but in the last 36 races, I've won 28!" said another with a proud flick of his tail.

Then they noticed a greyhound sitting in the corner. "I don't mean to boast," the greyhound said, "but out of 90 races, I've won 88!"

The horses looked at him in amazement. "Well," said one, "can you believe that—a talking dog!"

God's Creation

Three women were hiking in the mountains together and started talking about the beautiful scenery. That led to a discussion of God's marvelous world, and then to the animals He created, along with their distinguishing characteristics. The first posited that for friendship and loyalty, the dog wins, paws down. The second declared with a chuckle that no animal could beat the mule for obstinacy.

The third said: "I vote for the goose as the friendliest of all God's creatures." The others asked her how she had arrived at that conclusion.

"Because just a few minutes ago," she said, "a flock of geese flew right over us, and every single one of them honked and waved."

•

A young fellow going on his first African safari was confident he could handle any situation that might arise. Hoping to impress the experienced guide with his knowledge, he said, "I know that carrying a flashlight keeps the lions away."

"That's true in some cases," replied the guide. "It all depends on how fast you run while you're carrying the flashlight."

At Home

As usual, Timmy came thundering down the stairs, much to his dad's annoyance. Finally his dad, sitting downstairs, had had enough of the racket. "Timmy!" he shouted, "it's time you learn to use the stairs quietly! Now go back up and come down like a civilized person."

Obediently Timmy went back upstairs. Blissful silence followed, and then the boy appeared in front of his father. "Much, much better," his father said. "Now in the future, I want you to come down stairs just like that."

The boy broke into a happy smile. "Oh good!" he enthused, "because I slid down the railing!"

•

Sarah approached her parents one evening and asked if they would give her some money. Her mom and dad looked at each other, and then Mom said, "Sarah, it's time you learned the value of a dollar."

"I know the value of a dollar," the girl protested, "and that's why I'm asking for twenty."

Help!

The new father of twins was distressed about the escalating household expenses. Suddenly, everything was double—food, nursery furniture, clothes, doctor's visits. On one particular day he complained at length to his wife about the money she had spent on toiletries, including the cost of a canister of baby powder that she was using to prevent diaper rash. She heard him out, and then said calmly: "Let me remind you, dear...talc is cheap."

•

After students had turned in their essays, the teacher asked them to sign a paper stating that they had received no outside assistance. One student raised his hand and said, "I don't know if I can sign this, because I prayed for God's help with this assignment."

The teacher picked up that student's essay and studied it for several minutes. Then the teacher looked up and said, "You can go ahead and sign the paper with a clear conscience. I'm sure God heard your prayer, but looks like he chose to let you do this one all by yourself."

At Retail

The salesperson in the electronic store told his customer: "I guarantee this computer will do half your work for you."

"That's great," the customer said. "I'll take two!"

•

Rosie was shopping at a farmers market and spied a basket of oranges. "How much are these oranges?" she asked the farmer.

"Two for a quarter," he replied.
Picking up two, she examined them and then asked, "How much for just this one?"

"Fifteen cents," the farmer answered.

"Fine. Then I'll take this other one."

HOLY HUMOR

Irate, the woman called her local newspaper office. "Where's my Sunday paper?" she demanded.

"Ma'am," said the customer service rep, "today is Saturday. The Sunday paper will be delivered tomorrow, on Sunday."

A long pause followed. "Well," said the woman, much subdued, "that explains why no one showed up for church this morning."

•

A boy was waiting for his mom to come out of a store when a man approached him. The man asked, "Son, can you tell me the way to the post office?"

"Sure," replied the boy, "just turn right at the end of this block and it's right there."

"Thank you," said the man. "I'm the new pastor at the church on Vine Street, and I'd like to invite you and your family to come to church on Sunday. I'll show you the way to heaven."

"Sure," said the boy with a chuckle, "when you don't even know the way to the post office!"

UH-OH.

Once there was a boy who lived on a farm that had no indoor plumbing. He hated the outhouse because it was hot in the summer, cold in the winter, and stank all year round.

The facility stood near the banks of a small creek, and the boy liked to picture it falling into the water and floating away. Then one day after a particularly heavy spring rain had swollen the creek, he couldn't resist: he pushed the rickety structure into the creek and watched it disappear in the rushing water.

That evening his dad sternly ordered him to come into the den and sit down. Though he knew he was in trouble, he innocently asked why his father wanted to see him. "Someone pushed the outhouse into the creek," Dad said. "It was you, wasn't it?"

The boy hung his head and admitted that it was. "But," he added hastily, "remember that when George Washington chopped down the cherry tree, he didn't get in trouble because he told the truth!"

"When George Washington chopped down the cherry tree," Dad said, "his father wasn't in it."

Holy Humor

A woman who lived next door to the parsonage noticed that the preacher's personality at home was quite different from his personality at church. At home, he was shy, quiet, soft-spoken, and retiring. At church, however, he delivered loud, passionate, fire-and-brimstone sermons, rousing the congregation in the name of God.

One day she asked him about the dramatic transformation that occurred when he got into the pulpit. "Ah," he said, "that's my altar ego."

•

One Sunday morning, a pastor, known for his lengthy sermons, noticed that one man got up and left the service before he was finished preaching. Then, shortly before the sermon ended, the man returned to his pew. At the end of the service, the pastor asked the man why he had left mid-sermon. "I needed to get a haircut," the man said.

"Why didn't you do that before the service?" the pastor asked.

"Because I didn't need one at that point."

Hold on a Minute!

A young fellow was alone in his first apartment, and he thought that a pet would make the place less lonely. He didn't want a dog or cat, however—he had his mind on something unusual. After a discussion with the owner of a nearby pet store, he bought a centipede, along with a little white box for its house.

The fellow took his new pet to his apartment, found a good location for the centipede's box, and settled the critter inside. Next morning, the fellow peeked inside the box and said, "I'm going out to grab a cup of coffee. Want to come with me?"

When he didn't get an answer, he was concerned, so he put his face up to the door of the box and again said, "I'm going out to grab a cup of coffee. Want to come with me?" Still no answer.

Worried now, he again put his face up to the door of the box and shouted: "Hey, in there! I'm going out to grab a cup of coffee. Want to come with me?"

"I heard you the first time!" responded a little voice from inside the box. "Please wait a minute while I put on my shoes!"

"So long for now!"